The Color Nature Library
ROSES

By
JACQUELINE SEYMOUR

Designed by
DAVID GIBBON

Produced by
TED SMART

CRESCENT BOOKS

INTRODUCTION

A quick glance through the pictures in this book will show a number of apparently rather different flowers which can nevertheless be recognised quite confidently as roses. Wild roses have five petals; some of the roses shown here have ten times that or more. The existence of these other forms is almost entirely due to man's affection for the rose, which seems to have been constant throughout history. The esteem in which the rose was held meant that it was desirable enough to be deliberately cultivated. Such cultivation inevitably led, because of the proximity of dissimilar plants, to the unintentional as well as the intentional development of hybrids. In any case roses in their natural state have a tendency to double their flowers, produce colour variations and to hybridise. If any such variation appeared particularly attractive it would have been cultivated and so preserved.

The history of the rose is a long one. Fossilised roses have been found which are thirty million years old. Their more recent history is complicated and confused. The Persians cultivated roses, taking them with them to the lands they conquered. In ancient Greece the cult of the rose was widespread; the custom of strewing roses over graves originated there. The rose was dedicated to Aphrodite, goddess of love, and later to Eros. Both the Greeks and the Romans used it for garlands at their feasts and roses were used most lavishly at banquets celebrating victories. Roman warriors were frequently crowned with wreaths of roses and their women used the petals to scent their baths. The expression 'sub rosa' dates from Roman times. The rose suspended above the banqueting table meant that anything said was in strictest confidence; this prevented advantage being taken of verbal indiscretions made by diners in their cups. More recently the rose was carved or painted over confessionals and old Council Chambers, again symbolising discretion.

Roses were highly regarded by the Phoenicians and the Egyptians. Cleopatra provided beds of roses for honoured guests; the petals were also used for stuffing pillows and for strewing inches deep on floors.

The excesses of the later part of the Roman Empire together with strong links with Venus, patron of flower-gardens as well as goddess of love, brought the rose into ill-repute, and, albeit only briefly, it became a symbol of vice and licentiousness. The rose was condemned by the papacy as a heathen flower but affection for, and attachment to, the rose remained and the red rose came to symbolise Jesus' blood and the blood of the Christian martyrs; the white rose represented the purity of the Virgin Mary.

Roses have been grown in China since about 900 AD although the first China rose did not reach the West until the eighteenth century. The East is rich in wild species; the rose was therefore an obvious choice for cultivation in the Emperors' beautiful gardens.

Besides being a symbol of love the rose has also been a symbol of war. In the Wars of the Roses in Britain between 1455 and 1485 *Rosa gallica* was adopted as the red rose emblem of the House of Lancaster and the semi-double *Rosa alba* was the white rose symbolising the House of York. The two warring factions were united by the marriage of Henry Tudor and Elizabeth of York; the two roses were combined to form the red and white Tudor rose which remains a symbol of royalty to this day.

The dividing date between the so-called Old Roses and the modern varieties is generally taken to be 1800. During the early part of the nineteenth century the Empress Josephine's collection of roses at Malmaison made rose-growing a fashionable hobby in France. This fashion had an obvious effect on French nurserymen and many new roses were raised. Josephine's patronage of the artist Redouté has given us his well-known and beautiful paintings. It is said that during the Napoleonic Wars roses were sent to her from England and, having been given a special free conduct, they reached her safely. The China rose had reached Britain by this time, making the British products particularly attractive.

The art (and science) of rose breeding hinges on a particular and very inconvenient attribute of modern roses. They do not breed true. This means that if, for example, a Peace flower is fertilised by Peace pollen the resulting seedlings will all be different from each other and none will be identical to the parents. The reasons for this lie partly in the long history of the cultivation of the rose – so many characters have been incorporated over the centuries that the genetic make-up has become very complicated. The result, for all practical purposes, is that, in order to retain their particular characteristics, all new roses have to be propagated vegetatively; this is done by a process known as budding. Essentially what happens is that the root system and part of the stem of one established plant is used to grow the leaves and flowers of the desired variety, which develop from a single bud grafted onto such understock. Only one 'eye' from the new rose is needed to produce a whole plant which is a great advantage when dealing with a new or scarce cultivar. So, perhaps surprisingly, every single Peace rose bush has been produced vegetatively from one particular original seedling; all these plants are genetically identical.

Most new varieties of rose are produced by sexual and not vegetative reproduction, although new varieties do arise following spontaneous vegetative changes; these are called sports. The hybridist, however, is concerned with producing new plants from seed and he usually has to perform thousands of crosses in order to obtain one rose of marketable quality. These crosses are done in carefully controlled conditions so that he knows exactly which pollen has been used to fertilise which flower. The stamens from the female parent have to be removed to prevent self-pollination. Pollination is carried out by hand with the selected pollen and the flower then has to be protected from any further cross-pollination by such agents as bees or wind.

Gardeners who grow roses have plants which provide beauty and elegance with a minimum of labour; the labours of the hybridist in order to achieve this happy state are, by contrast, immense.

Facing page: Roses growing at Monza, Italy.

3

The exact number of species of wild rose, *Rosa*, which exist has been the subject of controversy in the past, largely because of the existence of many naturally occurring hybrids. It is now generally accepted that there are about one hundred and twenty distinct species, only a few of which have made an important contribution to the rose varieties that we know today. One of these is the Dog Rose, *Rosa canina*, shown in flower, *left,* and in bud, *right*; the fruits, hips or heps, are a conspicuous scarlet and an attractive oval shape, *below*. A possible origin of the name is that the Greeks and Romans believed that it could heal dog bites. This species is native to north Europe including Britain. Interestingly no wild rose species has ever been found south of the equator; introduced varieties flourish, particularly in countries like Australia and New Zealand.

It has long been the practice to bud roses; this is the process which allows nurserymen to raise plants cheaply and quickly. The Dog Rose has been extensively used as understock for budding although other species are now becoming popular for this purpose.

The Scotch or Burnet Rose or Scotch Brier, *Rosa spinosissima*, *left*, was known before 1600 when it could be found in north Europe and eastwards to Siberia. Wilhelm Kordes, working in Germany, has used its hardy qualities in his breeding programme resulting in his famous range of 'Spring' roses (Frühlingsanfang is shown on page 26.)

The Sweet Brier or Eglantine, *R. rubiginosa* or *R. eglanteria*, *right*, is another species native to north Europe including Britain. It is noted for its longevity and its fragrant leaves. The Penzance Sweet Briers are most often seen in gardens. These were created by Lord Penzance in the 1890s by crossing the Sweet Brier with other roses. The variety he named Lady Penzance is shown, *below*.

Rosa rubrifolia, below and left, has not been used much by hybridists. This native to central Europe is cultivated mainly for its beautiful foliage and hips.

R. moyesii came from north-west China. The flowers are blood-red and the flagon-shaped hips, *above,* are particularly attractive.

The Austrian Copper Brier, *R. foetida bicolor, right,* is a sport (a new variety which arises as a result of a naturally occurring mutation of the vegetative cells) of *R. foetida,* a native to north Iran and Kurdistan. It appears in the pedigrees on many well-known roses, including that of Peace.

Alba roses are among the most spectacular of all the Old Roses. Although the name suggests that they are white this is something of a misnomer as there are cream Alba roses as well as some in shades of pink. The original Alba rose was white and was adopted as an emblem by the House of York, but it was known long before the Wars of the Roses being grown by both the Greeks and the Romans. It is cultivated to this day in Bulgaria as one of the ingredients for making the perfume Attar of Roses. Alba roses all have the original *R. x alba* in their ancestry and are characterised by their tall, robust, disease-resistant growth. Most have attractive greyish-green leaves and all are deliciously scented. These attributes make them popular garden plants. Two kinds are shown here: Maiden's Blush, *left,* and Céleste or Celestial, *below right.* Maiden's Blush is known to have been grown in the fifteenth century although its origin is obscure. It is frequently seen in paintings of around this time. It tends to be rather variable which has led to some forms being given names of their own, the most extravagant of which is

Cuisse de Nymphe Emue (Thigh of the Passionate Nymph).

Céleste has narrow pointed buds which open into cup-shaped clear pink flowers. Its origin is unknown but it is reputed to have been picked by the British troops after the defeat of the French at Minden in 1759; it is therefore also known as the Minden Rose.

De Meaux, *below left*, and Tour de Malakoff, *right*, are both Centifolia roses. The original *R. x centifolia* has a number of names – Cabbage Rose, Provence Rose, Hundred-leaved Rose, Rose des Peintres. It was formerly believed to be very old but now it is thought to owe its origin to the work of Dutch nurserymen from about 1600 onwards. It is sterile; most of the cultivated varieties have arisen as sports.

The scented flowers of the rose De Meaux resemble miniature pompoms; the whole plant is small, growing to about half the height of the other Centifolia roses. It is believed to have been raised in 1789. Tour de Malakoff grows to a height of nearly two metres (six feet) which is more typical of Centifolias. The flowers change colour noticeably as they age being vivid carmine with edges of lilac when young, becoming bluer and heavily veined with violet and then fading to violet grey.

Gallica roses all display the influence of *Rosa gallica*, the French Rose, which is probably the most ancient of all the cultivated roses; it was known in temple gardens in 1200 BC.

Rosa Mundi or Versicolor, *left,* was first recorded in the sixteenth century although it had probably appeared before this. The belief that it was named after the 'fair Rosamund', Henry II's mistress, who died in 1176, probably has its roots in legend rather than in fact.

Deep colours and marbling and shading are typical of the Gallicas, which are once-only flowerers blooming in early summer. Cardinal de Richelieu, *below,* is much more violet than a cardinal's robes; the ball-shaped flowers darken with age to a deep purple.

The Bourbon roses arose quite by chance on the Ile de Bourbon, now called Réunion, as a cross between a Pink China and an Autumn Damask. They combine the best characteristics of the two, being robust, perpetual flowering and strongly scented. Madame Pierre Oger, *right,* was discovered in 1878, the sport of another Bourbon Rose, La Reine Victoria.

Hybrid Perpetual roses were the favourites of the Victorian age becoming popular before the Hybrid Teas. Souvenir du Docteur Jamain, *above*, was produced in 1865 and is considered by many to have the best scent of any rose, this being strong, sweet and rich.

Paul Neyron, *bottom right*, is a Hybrid Perpetual rose first produced in 1869. It has huge deep pink flowers but only a slight scent.

Buff Beauty, *top right*, is a Hybrid Musk rose introduced in 1939; it was probably bred by the Rev. J. Pemberton (see page 16). It has a stro scent. The flowers first appear in la June and if the weather is favourab they can still be seen at Christmas tim

The Hybrid Musk roses were large created by the Rev. J. H. Pemberton the years between 1912 and 1939. Li many other rose-lovers he was attracte to roses at an early age; he subsequent became an exhibitor. Although the flowers he exhibited were mainly large Hybrid Teas he was aware of the nee for roses which would be particular suitable for smallish gardens; that is say roses which needed little attentic while at the same time producing a l of flowers. He aimed to produ fragrant flowers borne on shrubs rath than on bedding plants. The Hybr Musk roses he produced are on distantly related to the Musk Ros *Rosa moschata*. Moonlight, *right,* was o of the first roses he produced. The lemo cream flowers with attractive golde stamens grow in large clusters througho the summer. Penelope, *below,* is anoth of Pemberton's creations, probably th most popular of them all. The flowe are pale pink when young but they fad to almost white as they age; they a strongly scented. Amazingly, Pen berton was not considered a larg grower for those days – he had abo four thousand trees!

Will Scarlet, *left,* is a modern Hybr Musk rose (1950) named after one Robin Hood's merry men.

The China Rose, *Rosa chinensis,* is a vigorous climbing rose, native, as it name suggests, to China. Roses were probably cultivated in China from about AD 900 but the results of this activity did not reach the West until about 1800 when Slater's Crimson China and Parson's Pink China arrived in England by way of India. These, and others which subsequently came from China, contributed the property of recurrent flowering, a very important part of the make-up of so many of our modern roses. Unfortunately most of these early imports were not hardy enough to survive a less hospitable climate and many of them are no more.

Little White Pet, *left,* is a recurrent flowering *R. chinensis* hybrid whose flower buds are attractively tinged with red.

Viridiflora, *below,* is probably a *R. chinensis* sport and a most unusual one with its green and purplish flowers.

F. J. Grootendorst, *right,* is a Rugosa rose (see page 20) which grows into a big prickly bush with a large number of relatively small scentless flowers.

Rugosa roses are among the toughes and hardiest members of the ros family. *Rosa rugosa*, the Ramanas Ros comes from northern Asia – Chin Japan and Korea. Rugosa roses a dense and bushy, early-flowering, wit apple-green foliage. *R. rugosa* itself little grown as a garden plant now, but has been used frequently as understoc

Sarah Van Fleet, *left*, is a vigorous *rugosa* hybrid, introduced in the Unite States in 1926, which is partic larly valuable if a dense hedge or scree is required. Its semi-double china-pir flowers have a delicious scent.

Roseraie de l'Hay, *below left*, is Rugosa rose produced by Coche Cochet in France at the turn of th century. It has very large richly-scente deep crimson-purple flowers whic develop from long-pointed scrolle buds. It rarely produces hips.

Frau Dagmar Hartopp, *below*, is als known as Fru Dagmar Hastrup. This a *R. rugosa* seedling introduced in 191 It has unusually large beautiful tomat shaped hips.

Pink Grootendorst, *right*, is a sport F. J. Grootendorst pictured on th previous page. While having an abui dance of bright pink flowers it is rath less vigorous than its parent.

Confusingly, the rose called Alba is not an Alba rose but a Rugosa rose; a white form of *Rosa rugosa*. The flowers, *left*, and the hips, *below*, are often borne at the same time. The single pure white flowers have golden-brown stamens. The large flask-shaped hips change from bright vermilion to orange-scarlet as they mature. The plant is a vigorous spreading shrub with the typical Rugosa apple-green leaves; these turn a rich gold in autumn.

Modern roses are considered on the following pages. Those illustrated here are called Modern Shrubs.

Scharlachglut or Scarlet Fire, *left*, was raised by Kordes and introduced in 1952. It is a very vigorous, very thorny, shrub or pillar rose with unscented single velvety flowers. The large pear-shaped hips are frost-resistant and provide a superb long-lasting display in autumn.

Golden Wings, *right and below*, was introduced four years after Scharlachglut by R. Shepherd of the United States. Its beautiful stamens are a most attractive feature, as is shown in the close-up picture. The large fragrant flowers are a clear light yellow fading to creamy white with age. They are pictured here with a Speckled Bush Cricket resting on them. The plant produces orange-red hips in autumn.

More Modern Shrubs are shown here. Frühlingsanfang, *top left*, is one of the extremely successful 'Spring' roses raised by Kordes. It is early flowering and produces maroon-red hips in autumn.

White Wings, *bottom left*, like Golden Wings on the previous page, has very beautiful stamens. The centres of the flowers of Ballerina, *below*, are again an attractive feature. These are white, the outer parts of the petals being a delicate pink. This rose was originally called a Hybrid Musk and it could have been one raised by Pemberton; certainly it has a slight musky scent.

Nymphenburg, *left*, is another Kordes rose, introduced in 1955. This vigorous, finely-scented, modern shrub can also be grown as a pillar rose. The large flowers vary in colour; the buds are apricot-pink but open into salmon-pink flowers with yellow centres and reddish edges. They fade in bright sunlight and as they age. Nymphenburg flowers very freely and is recurrent.

Constance Spry, *below*, is a modern rose introduced in 1961 but it has some of the characteristics of old fashioned varieties, the most noticeable of which is the flower shape. The leaves are unusual as they have only three leaflets. Constance Spry has a strong perfume and does not repeat flower. It was raised by D. Austin of England and is an appropriate memorial for the great rose-lover after whom it is named.

Raubritter, *right,* is yet another rose from the Kordes nurseries. It is free-flowering but blooms rather late in the season, the first buds opening at about mid-summer. It is not recurrent.

Nevada, *below,* was raised by Pedro Dot of Spain and named after the Sierra Nevada. It is rather an old shrub rose which was introduced in 1927. Despite its age it is extremely vigorous and free-flowering. It has pink-tinted buds which open into very large single creamy-white flowers which may themselves become pinkish in hot weather.

Climbing and rambling roses are the nearest in habit to the wild roses; the latter tend to grow in shady places, reaching the sunlight by means of their hooked thorns which lodge the stems into neighbouring bushes and trees.

Purity, *left*, is particularly valuable for growing up an old tree; it has extremely long, thorny rambling stems. The large pure white flowers are sweetly scented but it is only slightly recurrent.

Albertine, *right*, is a very popular large-flowered rambler. The dark coppery-pink flowers are strongly scented. They fade to a paler pink.

American Pillar, *below*, is another popular rambler especially suitable for growing on a rose arch or pergola. The flowers grow in large clusters but are not scented or recurrent.

These three are all fairly old roses having been introduced in 1917, 1921 and 1902 respectively.

31

he two roses on these pages are fairly
cent introductions. The lemon-
ented Golden Showers, *left*, was
troduced in the United States in 1956.
will reach nearly four metres (twelve
et) in a sheltered position; in less

favourable places it grows to about half
this. Golden Showers is one of the most
recurrent roses of all. The flat flowers
are large, double and pleasantly
fragrant; the buds are pointed.

Pink Perpétue, *above*, was raised by

C. Gregory & Sons Ltd. in England and
introduced in 1965. This is also a
recurrent blooming variety with an
unusually large number of flowers
being produced in the autumn.

33

Sympathie, *left*, was introduced by Kordes in 1964. As is the modern trend the flowers are of the hybrid tea type, each one has forty-three petals. They are pleasantly scented.

Mermaid, *below*, is another old climber; it was first introduced in 1918 and is perhaps the best known and the best loved of all the climbing roses. It is a robust repeat-flowering plant, evergreen in mild conditions, growing up to about nine metres (thirty feet). It is sterile and so never produces any hips.

Crimson Conquest, *right*, is particularly suited to be grown as a pergola rose. It has rather small flowers. Its age lies between those of Sympathie and Mermaid – it was introduced in 1931.

The method by which roses climb using their thorns has already been mentioned. The thorns of different roses vary in size, shape, colour and number. Their distribution varies too; thorns may be borne on the main stem but can also be found on the tiny common stems shared by the leaflets. Some varieties have a plentiful supply of thorns on these stems and none on the main ones. Some thorns are very beautiful. The thorn on the stem of Climbing Lady Hillingdon, *left*, is an example of this beauty; the picture also shows the purplish tinges typical of young shoots of this variety. The rose is a sport of the tea rose Lady Hillingdon. The flowers are double, creamy yellow in colour with a darker centre. They tend to be rather pendulous and are strongly tea-scented.

Danse du Feu, *below*, is also called Spectacular. It was raised by C Mallerin in France. Besides looking attractive when grown up a wall, as shown in the picture, it makes an extremely effective weeping standard. One does not have to read very much on the subject before becoming aware that the name of Wilhelm Kordes is a significant one in the world of rose breeding. His father had a general nursery and the son studied in

Germany, Switzerland and France, eventually starting his own business in England. This was ruined by World War I; he was interned during this period. Returning to Germany he was forced to start from scratch, and because of the difficult climate in Holstein where he was working he decided to aim for hardiness and disease resistance. He has given his name to a new species, *Rosa kordesii*, which arose from a normally infertile hybrid. This was one of the parents of Leverkusen, *above*, a climber or pillar he introduced in 1954. Maigold, *right*, is another Kordes rose. It reflects another of his favourite breeding lines, that containing the Scotch or Burnet Rose, *R. spinosissima*, which appears as a parent of all the 'Frühling' roses. A disadvantage of this strain is that they are all very thorny; this is something that the firm of Kordes, now controlled by Wilhelm's son, Reimer, is trying to improve on.

Hybrid Tea roses are large-flowered shapely bedding and exhibition roses which can be obtained in a wide range of vivid colours and bicolours. The first hybrid teas were obtained by crossing hybrid perpetuals with the tea-scented roses. A selection of hybrid tea roses follows; some are fairly recent additions to the catalogues, some are established favourites and a few have become less popular although all can still be found growing in gardens.

Left, Dr. A. J. Verhage, also known as Golden Wave. Rose Gaujard, *below*, and *right*, Virgo, also called Virgo Liberationem.

Belle Blonde

June Park

Tradition

Tiffany

Ernest H. Morse

Pink Favourite

Golden Giant

Candy Stripe

Diamond Jubilee

Super Star
Tropicana

La Jolla

Maria Callas
Miss All-American Beauty

a

Cleopatra

Kordes' Perfecta

ova

Invitation

Red Devil
Coeur d'Amour

ion

Memoriam

Percy Thrower

on Churchill

Gold Crown

Champs Elysées

The beautiful geranium-red rose, *below*, was raised by another well-known German breeder, Mathias Tantau. It is called Duftwolke, Fragrant Cloud or Nuage Parfumé; the last two are literal translations. Mathias Tantau senior, father of the present owner of the nursery, began the business in Holstein in 1906. At the end of World War II Mathias Tantau junior took over the firm, and, like so many other European breeders, found that breeding had to be started again from practically nothing. Super Star (page 40), called Tropicana in the United States, is undoubtedly his biggest success. It won the most coveted prizes in the year 1960 and joins Peace as one of the best-selling roses of all time. Super Star is the result of crosses begun by his father as far back as 1937. Other prize-winning roses have been produced by Tantau regularly since 1954. They include Mainzer Fastnacht (Blue Moon), Duke of Windsor and Whisky Mac.

Far right, Pascali; *near right*, Mischief which has Peace as a parent; *below right* Avoca, raised by Alexander Dickson in 1907.

Alexander, *left*, was named after Field Marshal Earl Alexander of Tunis. Königin der Rosen, *right*, is called Queen of Roses in English. It is also known as Colour Wonder.

The story of the naming of the Meilland rose now most widely known as 'Peace', *below*, is a moving and romantic one. Antoine Meilland was the first member of the Meilland family to grow roses professionally, having had a burning ambition to do so from the age of eleven. He married the daughter of a tailor turned professional rose-grower, Claudia Dubreuil, who shared his devotion to roses, a passion that was inherited by their son, Francis. Francis' particular interest was hybridising and he created this particular rose which was first shown to professional rose-growers in June 1939. Just before normal communications were cut at the beginning of the Second World War small consignments of the budded rose were dispatched to a rose grower in Germany, a second in Italy and a third in the United States. In fact the last package left, thanks to the help of the American Consul in Lyons, on the very last clipper to leave for North America.

Because of the problems of communication none of the recipients of these parcels knew that the family had

unanimously decided to call the rose Madame A. Meilland in memory of Claudia, who had died at the tragically early age of forty, to whom they all owed so much and who had been particularly beloved. The family heard later that their German client had grown the rose in his own garden and was so delighted with it that he had named it Gloria Dei (Glory of God) later still they learnt that the Italian had named his Gioia (Joy). But there was no news at all of the parcel sent to America. It was not until after the war that they heard that the rose was named 'Peace' at a special Name Giving Ceremony on April 29th, 1945. So a lovely rose has four beautiful names, of which 'Peace' particularly caught the mood of the time. Sales have been enormous. In 1954 it was estimated that over thirty million had been sold. Harry Wheatcroft estimated more recently that sales were around one hundred million. This rose is still as vigorous and robust as ever. It has enormous well-shaped blooms each composed of forty-five petals which shade from ivory to pale gold fringed with a delicate pink.

Left, My Love. *Below,* Montezuma raised by H. C. Swim in the U.S.A.

am McGredy has said that the most
popular colour for roses is scarlet red
followed by vermilion, yellow, pink,
white and shades of lavender, in that
order. The position of yellow so high on
the list is an interesting one; in the
language of flowers the yellow rose
signifies infidelity and falsehood! The
search for a blue rose continues,
although the attraction lies more in its
curiosity value than in its expected
beauty. One of the best results of
breeding with this in mind is Tantau's
very-lilac Mainzer Fastnact, *right*, also
called Blue Moon and Sissi. The desire
for a blue rose is a relatively recent one.
1925 Alexander Dickson III raised a
'blue' seedling which was so severely
criticised that his father insisted on
destroying all the plants. Something
rather similar happened in the
McGredy nursery when Sam McGredy
discarded and burnt a similar
seedling which he considered worth-
less.

Above, Buccaneer, another Swim
rose.

Criterion

Doreen

Lady Seton

Beauté

Pink Supreme

Whisky Mac

Eden Rose

Grand'mère Jenny

Wendy Cussons

Sultane

Manuela

Princess

i
n Prince

Hector Deane

Isabel de Ortiz

Debat

Brandenburg

Message

Highness
che Hoheit

Papa Meilland

Pink Peace

treet

The Doctor

Duke of Windsor
Herzog von Windsor

49

Producing a new rose is an extreme time-consuming hit-and-miss affa The processes involved include han pollinating, rearing seedlings, assessi these plants, budding and reassessir all this can take from seven to ten yea J. L. Harkness' report on his breedir programme gives an idea of the tedio and time-consuming work that involved. In the summer of 1963 he ma about seven-and-a-half thousar crosses. The same number of see from these crosses were sown in ea 1964. (The fact that these numbe are the same is coincidental. A ferti cross will yield a number of seeds in tl hip – an infertile one naturally produc none). Seventy-three of these seedlin were retained for further trial, but or eighteen of these were still bei studied in late 1967. No doubt most these were subsequently rejected. It therefore obvious that breedir involves unlimited patience as well skill, knowledge and inspiration; addition success depends a good d on luck.

Uncle Walter, *left*, and Piccadil *right*, are both products of the McGre nursery. *Below left*, Picture; *below ri* Helen Traubel.

Floribunda roses are repeat-flowering cluster roses used for bedding purposes. A number of different varieties are shown on the following pages. They were formerly called Hybrid Polyanthas and have arisen from a line first produced by D. Poulsen in Denmark, obtained when he crossed dwarf bedding roses known as Polyantha Pompoms with Hybrid Teas. At first plants with single flowers growing in clusters were produced. Now free-flowering forms have won universal popularity and the trend for the last twenty years or so has been to obtain floribunda roses with blooms of the hybrid tea type.

The three roses illustrated here are of this form. Tony Jacklin, *left*, Queen Elizabeth, *right*, and Arthur Bell, *below*. Queen Elizabeth has become particularly popular; with its massive growth frequently reaching two metres (over six feet) it is more shrub-like than most floribundas. The flowers are borne both singly and in trusses.

Bonfire Night, *right*, is a floribunda rose produced at the outstandingly successful McGredy nurseries in Northern Ireland. Sam McGredy IV is the present owner of the business; his father died when he was two years old. In the years before he was able to take over the firm himself it was run by his uncle, Walter Johnson, after whom he named the rose Uncle Walter. Sam McGredy too had to start again with a greatly reduced breeding stock after the last war but has achieved a large number of successes including Elizabeth of Glamis, Piccadilly, Picasso, City of Leeds and Lady Seton (the married name of Julia Clements). He has always advocated collaboration between hybridists and numbers several of them among his closest friends; he and Reimer Kordes in particular exchange information about their breeding programmes. He has long considered that New Zealand has the perfect climate for rose-growing and is now living and working there.

Left, Woburn Abbey; Schneewitchen, *below*, is literally translated as Snow White but it is called Iceberg in Britain and Fée des Neiges in France.

Charleston, *left*, is another Meillan rose, and a very striking one; the youn petals are yellow flushed with crimson eventually they all become crimson Orangeade, *below*, is a single bright orange floribunda.

Because of the large number involved new roses are not usuall named until their trials have prove them worthy of inclusion in th catalogues; in order to identify then they are given numbers by the breeder The number generally indicates th number of the cross, the year, etc. Peace for example, was numbered 3-35-4C Some breeders, Sam McGredy is one give their promising roses nickname but for most the naming process start in earnest when the rose has prove itself a marketable possibility. Rose have long been named for com memorative, complimentary or senti mental reasons, or given names that wi fire the public's imagination: onl relatively recently has sponsorshi become an accepted part of the rose breeding scene.

From the earliest days hybridist have named roses after their familie friends and well-known people, and th practice continues. Grand'mère Jenn and Uncle Walter are example

included in this book of modern breeders honouring members of their own families. The roses Queen Elizabeth, Elizabeth of Glamis, Duke of Windsor, Winston Churchill and Alexander are all named after famous people and there are many more dedicated in this way. A large number of roses have descriptive names, of which the best convey both the type of rose and its desirability. Some examples included in these pages are Virgo, Fragrant Cloud, My Love, Blue Moon, Message, Picture, Piccadilly and Orangeade. Of commercial names, Arthur Bell is one included in this book; other very successful roses named in this way are Evelyn Fison, Mullard Jubilee and National Trust.

Kathleen Ferrier, *above,* is a richly-perfumed floribunda shrub. Picasso, *right,* represents a breakthrough in rose colouration. McGredy calls it 'hand-painted'; the petals are brilliant scarlet and snow white at the same time. It also reflects the trend for shorter roses.

Masquerade, *below,* is a floribunda showing an attractive series of colour changes as it ages. The flowers are yellow when young, becoming salmon-pink and then dark red.

The Fairy, *right,* is a dwarf floribunda of great charm; the present fashion is for smaller bushes but this one was first introduced as long ago as 1932.

While flower form and colour is usually of prime importance when choosing a rose, the leaves, thorns and hips all add to the beauty of the plant. Thorns and hips have already been illustrated and discussed, but little has been said about foliage. The general shape of the leaflets of a rose is oval but the shape of the oval itself varies. The characteristics of the serrations of the edge also vary. Some are large and prominent as in the Centifolias, but Rugosa roses have small, smooth, rounded teeth which hardly show because they are rolled under the leaf.

The surface of the leaves varies as well some are smooth and shiny, som downy. Most obvious of all, of course are the different colours that appear o rose leaves. These are most marked i the early stages of growth but th autumnal dying colours can also b very striking. Colours that can be see include various shades of red an bronze, purple and grey as well as a shades of green from dark olive t palest apple.

60

More floribunda roses – *top left*, City of Leeds; *bottom left*, Escapade; *top right*, Frensham; *bottom right*, Alison Wheatcroft.

Opinions differ widely about scent in roses, some people asserting that modern roses do not have the scents of the older varieties. It has been estimated, however, that about one third of the so-called Old Roses were scentless and the same applies to about the same proportion of modern roses. The Gallica roses have a really strong rose perfume but roses have a range of other scents. Musk roses smell rather like the musk obtained from the scent gland of the male Musk Deer. Tea roses have a fragrance reminiscent of tea. Other scents described include those of apples, apricots, lemons, raspberries and spices. It is quite possible to produce a rose with a really unpleasant smell – such a rose is rapidly disposed of by the hybridist. Certainly scent is, for most people, not an over-riding factor when choosing a rose; Peace and Super Star (Tropicana) are two of the best-selling roses in the world and neither is strongly fragrant.

The rose has been used for hundreds of years as a source of perfume. All kinds of properties have been ascribed to perfumes, including medicinal ones. Rose-water was used for fainting, trembling and shaking; roses were supposed to strengthen the heart and refresh the spirit. The petals boiled with white wine and herbs have been used in the treatment of gun-shot wounds. No doubt the scent was most valuable of all for disguising evil smells.

The Muslems used thousands of gallons of rose-water to purify each mosque after recapturing it from the Crusaders. There is some doubt about who actually started to distil rose-water first. The process was certainly known around 900 AD in Spain. The French, subsequently so famous for their perfume industry, did not adopt the technique until the early thirteenth century.

The essential oil of roses, Attar or Otto of Roses, is obtained by a different method. This strongly-perfumed oil is obtained by macerating the rose petals and infusing them in warm oil or melted fat. The resulting product is solid, only becoming liquid if warmed. The process was probably first used in the early seventeenth century. Bulgaria is still the greatest producer of oil of roses. The rose is important in the French perfume industry too; at Grasse its production is second only to that of jasmine.

61

Dopey, *left,* is one of a series of dwarf floribundas known as Compacta roses produced by G. de Ruiter. They are named after the seven dwarfs – the others are called Doc, Happy, Sleepy, Sneezy, Grumpy and Bashful.

Cricri, *below,* is a miniature raised by Francis Meilland. *Right,* a rose pergola in Pistoia, Italy.

Attractive flowers do not necessarily ensure that a rose is a commercial success. The rose also has to be disease resistant and hardy. The modern practice of sending roses to trial grounds in different parts of the country, and sometimes to different countries, has proved a valuable one in assessing how roses will perform in conditions different from those under which they were raised. As well as liability to disease, the size of the bloom and even its colour can be affected by different climates. The breeder thus obtains invaluable information about his roses; in Britain and on the Continent their performance is assessed by impartial experts.

The miniature roses on this page illustrate the current trend in the rose industry.

INDEX

First published in Great Britain 1978 by
Colour Library International Ltd.
Designed by David Gibbon.
Produced by Ted Smart.
© Text: Jacqueline Seymour
© Illustrations: CLI/Bruce Coleman Ltd.
Colour separations by La Cromolito, Milan, Italy.
Display and Text filmsetting by
Focus Photoset, London, England.
Printed and bound by Group Poligrafici Calderara - Bologna - Italy
Published by Crescent Books,
a division of Crown Publishers Inc.
All rights reserved.
Library of Congress Catalogue Card No. 78-50082
CRESCENT 1978